Kingdom Curriculum for Kids: God's Image

By Gena Matthews

Kingdom Curriculum for Kids

ISBN— 9798652446925

© 2020 REIGN Worldwide, Inc.

REIGN Worldwide Publications

For more information about REIGN Worldwide, Inc. and its products call 1-888-800-4896 or visit www.reignworldwide.org or visit www.genamatthews.com.

All Scripture quotations, unless noted otherwise, are from the Holy Bible, *King James Version.*

Scripture quotations marked (AMP) are taken from the *Amplified Bible,* Copyright 1954, 1958, 1962, 1964, 1965, 1987 by the Lockman Foundation. Used by permission.

Definitions marked *Strong's* are from *The New Strong's Expanded Exhaustive Concordance of the Bible,* Thomas Nelson Publishers, Inc. Nashville, Tennessee.

Definitions marked *Webster's* are from *Merriam-Webster's Online Dictionary,* http://www.m-w.com/dictionary

All rights reserved. No part of this book may be reproduced in any form without permission in writing from the publisher, except in the case of brief quotations embodied in church related publications, critical articles or reviews.

© Copyright 2020 Gena Matthews

Introduction

The purpose of this book is to give youth a clear understanding of who they are from a Kingdom perspective. This clear understanding will assist them in navigating the challenges they will face in the times and culture that we live in today.

Acknowledgments

I thank God for another opportunity to expand the Kingdom Curriculum for Kids series. I want to thank my husband for all of his love, support and encouragement. I would like to thank my daughter Gena Nicole for her insight and help with the activities in the curriculum. I would also like to thank Cyrus Caisip for encouraging me to continue the KCK series.

TABLE OF CONTENT

LESSON 1	HOW TO ENTER GOD'S KINGDOM	6
LESSON 2	WHO ARE YOU?	11
LESSON 3	GOD'S ORIGINAL PLAN	16
LESSON 4	IMAGE OF CHRIST	22
LESSON 5	THE ENEMY CHALLENGES IDENTITY	26
LESSON 6	GOD'S ESTABLISHED PURPOSE FOR MAN ON EARTH	31
LESSON 7	GOD IS THE AUTHOR	35
LESSON 8	LAW OF LIKE KIND	41
LESSON 9	GOD'S ULTIMATE PURPOSE	48
LESSON 10	WHAT IS MAN?: GOD'S VOICE IN THE EARTH	54
LESSON 11	REPRESENTATION OF GOD	60
LESSON 12	NOT CONFORMING TO THE CURRENT CULTURE PT.1	64
LESSON 13	NOT CONFORMING TO THE CURRENT CULTURE PT.2	73

Kingdom Curriculum for Kids: God's Image

Lesson 1   How to enter God's Kingdom

- God has a Kingdom called Heaven.

- God wanted to expand His Kingdom and share it with man, so He created earth.

- God made the earth perfectly suited and ready for man to live on.

- Then God made man by speaking him into existence and placed man in the earth.

- He made them male and female.

- God gave man the ability to have any food grown in the earth, except the fruit of one tree.

- Adam and Eve made a choice to disobey God by eating the fruit that was forbidden.

- Adam and Eve lost God's Kingdom on earth as a result of their disobedience.

- In the fullness of time, God sent His Son Jesus to the earth to bring His Kingdom back into the earth.

- Jesus died and made the sacrifice that was necessary to cleanse man from his sin and to restore God's Kingdom back into the earth making it available to man again.

- In order for you to enter the Kingdom of God, you must receive Jesus as your Savior. You must believe that Jesus was born, lived a sinless life, died on the cross, was raised to life three days later, went back to Heaven, and is going to return to earth for all who received Him.

Questions for Lesson 1

1. What did God want to do with man?

_____
_____
_____

2. What did God do with the earth before He put man on it?

_____
_____
_____

3. How did God make mankind?

_____
_____
_____

4. What did God provide for man on earth?

_____
_____
_____

5. How did Adam and Eve lose the Kingdom?

_____
_____
_____

6. What did Jesus come to do?

_____

_____

_____

7. How did Jesus restore God's Kingdom?

_____

_____

_____

8. How can you enter the Kingdom of God?

_____

_____

_____

Art Project 1

Kingdom Curriculum for Kids: God's Image

Lesson 2   Who Are You?

- If you made the decision to receive Jesus as your Lord and Savior, you are now born into a new Kingdom and you are a citizen of that Kingdom.

- Kingdom citizenship comes with benefits and responsibilities.

- Because you are a Kingdom citizen, you have the right to be protected by God.

- You have the right to be provided for by God.

- You have the right to have your God given purpose fulfilled.

- Kingdom citizenship also makes you part of God's family. You become a son of God when you are born again.

- When there are reference to the word <u>man</u> and <u>son</u>, these words refer to position, not gender.

- The word <u>man</u> represents mankind in which there are males and female.

- The word <u>son</u> represents a family member in which there are sons and daughters.

- God specifically mentions when He made man, He made them, male and female. God made them that way on purpose in order to have both males and females fulfill specific purposes.

- Kingdom citizenship also comes with responsibility. As a Kingdom citizen, you are responsible for obeying the King, being loyal to the King and giving to the King's Kingdom.

- The Kingdom is not a welfare state, where God is always giving to you without receiving anything from you. God wants a relationship that is reciprocal. That means in this relationship, there is giving and receiving.

Questions for Lesson 2

1. When you become a Kingdom citizen, what are your rights?
   _____
   _____
   _____

2. What do you become in God's family?
   _____
   _____
   _____

3. What does the word <u>man</u> represent in the Kingdom of God?
   _____
   _____
   _____

4. What does the word <u>son</u> represent in the Kingdom of God?
   _____
   _____
   _____

5. Why did God make man male and female?
   _____
   _____
   _____

6. What are your responsibilities as a Kingdom citizen?
_____
_____
_____

7. What is a reciprocal relationship?
_____
_____
_____

Puzzle 1

```
a b c d e f g y h i j k l i m u
b n o p q r s a t u v w x m y n
c z a b c d e f g h i j a k d
d l m n o p q r r s t u v g w e
e x y z z a b e c d e c l e a r
w o r r o m o t h f g h i g j s
f r h o k l m s n o p q r s t t
g i i p u v i e w x y z a b c a
h g j q a f k y x f n d e f l n
i i c r e d a t y g a h i j i d
j n u s s d l c z o v c k l k i
k a l y o u t h m n i p e k e n
l l t t p e n a v i g a t i n g
m a u t r f m l q r a s t n e u
n s r u u q n l v w t x y g s z
o b e v p g o e a f e o n d s b
p c k m n o i n i m o d a o a c
q d l w i h p g b g k p l m d e
r e e v i t c e p s r e p w f g
s f m x b i q u c h l q t x h i
t g n y c j r v d i m r u y j k
u v w x y z s w e j n s v z l m
```

purpose
youth
clear
understanding
kingdom
perspective
navigating
challenge

face
times
culture
today
yesterday
tomorrow
image
original

likeness
dominion
fish
navigate
plan

Kingdom Curriculum for Kids: God's Image

Lesson 3   God's Original Plan

Genesis 1:26 KJV

"And God said, Let us make man in our image after our likeness: and let them have dominion over the fish of the sea, and over the fowl of the air, and over the cattle, and over all the earth, and over every creeping thing that creeps upon the earth."

- When we are learning lessons from the Bible, we must understand what God's original plan was for us.

- God wants us to have dominion over the earth.

- <u>Dominion</u> is God's authority, final authority and absolute authority.

- <u>Authority</u> is the right to do as you wish with what you have authority over.

- <u>God's Original Plan</u> for us is the manifestation of His Heavenly Kingdom here on earth in partnership with His sons and daughters.

- Manifestation is when something is perceptible or visible. When something manifests, you can experience it with your five senses.

- God made us like Him so that He could work with us and through us.

- God made us a spirit, with a soul (mind, will, emotions) and we live in a flesh body.

- Our flesh body is what we live in here on earth. This dirt body allows us to be legal on the dirt earth.

2 Corinthians 4:7 GWT

"Our bodies are made of clay, yet we have the treasure of the Good News in them. This shows that the superior power of this treasure belongs to God and doesn't come from us."

- Image and likeness of God is what qualifies man for dominion and gives man dominion in the earth.

- As sons and daughters of God, we act like God by speaking.

- *Genesis 2:7 "speaking spirit"*
  Onkelos https://www.sefaria.org/Onkelos--Genesis

John 1:1 BSB

"In the beginning was the Word, and the Word was with God, and the Word was God."

Psalm 89:27 BSB

"I will indeed appoint him as My firstborn, the highest of the kings of the earth."

Colossians 1:15 BSB

"The Son is the image of the invisible God, the firstborn over all creation."

Romans 8:29

"For those God foreknew, He also predestined to be conformed to the image of His Son, so that He would be the firstborn among many brothers."

Colossians 3:16a BSB

"Let the word of Christ richly dwell within you as you teach and admonish one another with all wisdom, …"

Questions for Lesson 3

1. What do we need to understand when we are learning from the Bible?
   _____
   _____
   _____

2. What is dominion?
   _____
   _____
   _____

3. What is authority?
   _____
   _____
   _____

4. What is God's original plan?
   _____
   _____
   _____

5. Why did God make us like Him?
   _____
   _____
   _____

6. What allows us to be legal on the earth?
_____
_____
_____

7. What qualifies us for dominion?
_____
_____
_____

Puzzle 2

A B C D E F G H I J K L M N O P Q R S T U V
1 2 3 4 5 6 7 8 9 10 11 12 13 14 15 16 17 18 19 20 21 22

W X Y Z   2 7 8 9
23 24 25 26   27 28 29 30

__ __ __ __ __   __ __ : __ __   __ __ __
16 19 1 12 13   29 30   27 28   2 19 2

" __   __ __ __ __   __ __ __ __ __
   9   23 9 12 12   9 14 4 5 5 4

__ __ __ __ __ __ __   __ __ __   __ __
1 16 16 15 9 14 20   8 9 13   1 19

__ __   __ __ __ __ __ __ __ __ __,
13 25   6 9 18 19 20 2 15 18 14

__ __ __   __ __ __ __ __ __   __ __
20 8 5   8 9 7 8 5 19 20   15 6

__ __ __   __ __ __ __ __   __ __
20 8 5   11 9 14 7 19   15 6

__ __ __   __ __ __ __ __."
20 8 5   5 1 18 20 8

21

Kingdom Curriculum for Kids: God's Image

Lesson 4   Image of Christ

Genesis 1:26a KJV

"And God said, Let us make man in our image, after our likeness; and let them have dominion..."

Genesis 9:6b BSB

"...for in His own image God has made mankind."

Romans 5:14b GWT

"...Adam is an image of the one who would come."

- We are the image of Christ who speaks for God in this world.
- We represent God to all of creation.

1 Corinthians 12:27 NIV

"Now you are the body of Christ, and each one of you is a part of it."

Psalm 8:5-6 NLT

"Yet you made them only a little lower than God and crowned them with glory and honor. You gave them charge of everything you made, putting all things under their authority."

- What is image?

- Image is a visual representation or exact likeness of something.

- Kingdom citizens are visual representations of God in the earth.

- What role does the image play?

- When people see us, they should see the image of God.

- We represent God in the earth. We reflect God in the earth.

- To be a representative of God means we can act on God's behalf.

- To be a reflection of God means that we bring the presence of God wherever we go.

2 Corinthians 3:18 NLT

"So all of us who have had that veil removed can see and reflect the glory of the Lord. And the Lord—who is the Spirit—makes us more and more like him as we are changed into his glorious image."

Questions for Lesson 4

1. Who are the representatives for God in the earth?
   _____
   _____
   _____

2. What is the definition of image?
   _____
   _____
   _____

3. What role does the image play?
   _____
   _____
   _____

4. What does it mean to be a representative of God?
   _____
   _____
   _____

5. What does it mean to be a reflection of God?
   _____
   _____
   _____

Art Project 2

Find the hidden crowns. Color the picture.

Kingdom Curriculum for Kids: God's Image

Lesson 5   The Enemy Challenges Identity

- Do you know who you are?

- The enemy is challenging the identity of the sons of God.

- Just like he challenged Eve in the Old Testament and Jesus in the New Testament, he is challenging us.

Genesis 3:1-5 BSB

*"Now the serpent was more crafty than any beast of the field that the LORD God had made. And he said to the woman, "Did God really say, 'You must not eat from any tree in the garden?'" The woman answered the serpent, "We may eat the fruit of the trees of the garden, but about the fruit of the tree in the middle of the garden, God has said, 'You must not eat of it or touch it, or you will die.'" "You will not surely die," the serpent told her.
"For God knows that in the day you eat of it, your eyes will be opened and you will be like God, knowing good and evil."*

Matthew 4:3-11 BSB

"The tempter came to Him and said, "If You are the Son of God, tell these stones to become bread." But Jesus answered, "It is written: 'Man shall not live on bread alone, but on every word that comes from the mouth of God.' " Then the devil took Him to the holy city and set Him on the pinnacle of the temple. "If You are the Son of God," he said, "throw Yourself down. For it is written: 'He will command His angels concerning You, and they will lift You up in their hands, so that You will not strike Your foot against a stone. "Jesus replied, "It is also written: 'Do not put the Lord your God to the test. " Again, the devil took Him to a very high mountain and showed Him all the kingdoms of the world and their glory. "All this I will give You," he said, "if You will fall down and worship me." "Away from Me, Satan!" Jesus declared. "For it is written: 'Worship the Lord your God and serve Him only.' Then the devil left Him, and angels came and ministered to Him."

- Knowing who you are allows you to overcome the attacks of the enemy.

- Eve did not know who she was, but Jesus did.

- We have to know how to engage this world and we need to know who we are to do it.

- The enemy tries to observe man's identity by causing man to question who he is.

- The enemy will use twisted doctrine to challenge you in your identity.

2 Timothy 3:5 NLT

"They will act religious, but they will reject the power that could make them godly. Stay away from people like that!"
Ephesians 4:14 NLT

Then we will no longer be immature like children. We won't be tossed and blown about by every wind of new teaching. We will not be influenced when people try to trick us with lies so clever they sound like the truth.

Questions for Lesson 5

1. Do you know who you are?
   _____
   _____
   _____

2. Who did not know their identity in the Garden of Eden?
   _____
   _____
   _____

3. Who came to earth to show us who we are?
   _____
   _____
   _____

4. Are you able to engage the world successfully if you do not know who you are?
   _____
   _____
   _____

5. What does the enemy use to challenge your identity?
   _____
   _____
   _____

Puzzle 3

```
a b d f h j a l e s s o n s l n
c c n a b e c d c e f g t h i j
e d o k s l m n n o p h q r s t
g e p u r v w x e y g n i h t z
i f q a e u h v i i a b c d e f
k g r b t y t i r o h t u a g h
m h s c h v i w e i j k l g m n
o h t d g w j x p o p q r n s t
p i t r u x k y x u v w x i y z
q g u p a r t n e r s h i p a b
r n v e d e l o z k p z c e d e
s i w r l y m i a l q f g e h i
t n x c m z n t b e r j k r l y
u r y e n a o a c l l m n c o l
v a z p o b p t d b s t p q r n
w e e t p c q s e i t s t t u e
x l f i q d r e f s u v w a x v
y j g b l w o f g i v r y z c a
z k h l r e s i n v i s i b l e
a l i e s f t n b m w o a a b h
e t u l o s b a i n x n c d e f
b m j k t g u m j o y s g h i j
```

sea
fowl
air
cattle
creeping
thing
earth
learning

absolute
authority
right
manifestation
heavenly
partnership
sons
daughters

visible
invisible
experience
lessons
perceptible

Kingdom Curriculum for Kids: God's Image

Lesson 6   God's Established Purpose for Man on Earth

- Man's partnership with God in manifesting His heavenly Kingdom on earth could not be accomplished without man being in God's <u>image</u> and <u>likeness</u>.

Genesis 1:26

"And God said, Let us make man in our image after our likeness: and let them have dominion over the fish of the sea, and over the fowl of the air, and over the cattle, and over all the earth, and over every creeping thing that creeps upon the earth."

- God established man's purpose in the earth to <u>creation</u> before man was placed in the earth.

- Whenever there is the absence of the image of God in a man's life, man reverts to ignorance.

- What is ignorance?

- Ignorance is the failure to recognize available facts and information. You ignore what is obvious.

- Man reverts to his fallen <u>imagination</u> to fashion his identity.

Romans 1:21 NLT

"Yes, they knew God, but they wouldn't worship him as God or even give him thanks. And they began to think up foolish ideas of what God was like. As a result, their minds became dark and confused."

Questions for Lesson 6

1. What does man possess from God that allows him to partner with God?

   _____
   _____
   _____

2. Who was God speaking to in Genesis 1:26?

   _____
   _____
   _____

3. What does man revert or turn to when God is not in his life?

   _____
   _____
   _____

4. What is ignorance?

   _____
   _____
   _____

5. What does fallen man use to fashion or shape his identity?

   _____
   _____
   _____

Puzzle 4

```
a v a b c d e f g h i j k l m n
b w o p q r d s t u v w x y z a
c x q l f n i h g f e d c b a b
d y r t i s r q p o n m l k j c
e z s m r u v a w x y z m a e d
f p t a s b c d p e f g l h i e
g o u p t o y n m p l l j i k f
h n v q b d r s t u o v w x v g
i h k r o w f d g w y i x z y e
j m i b r g e c n b a z n k a h
k l w g n i n n i g e b w t b i
l k x u h d l k k w m n i l c j
m j y h t e e l a x l r n m d k
n i z i g c s m e y i o d n e t
o h j a u b f t p p k p e o r l
p g l s v a y n s z j q e i f m
q f k r w f g o v e i r d r o w
r e l q i l h p u f n s v p g n
s d m l x e i q t g h s u q h o
t c a p y s n o i t o m e r i p
u u n o z h j r s u t u t s j q
q b a z y x w l l i w v u t s r
```

senses	live	appoint
work	dirt	firstborn
spirit	allow	highest
soul	legal	body
mind	qualify	indeed
will	speaking	
emotions	beginning	
flesh	word	

Kingdom Curriculum for Kids: God's Image

Lesson 7   God is the Author

- God is the Creator of Heaven and the earth. He spoke the universe into existence.

Psalm 33:9 CEV

"As soon as he spoke the world was created; at his command, the earth was formed."

- The world is experiencing problems that they do not have an answer for.

- The world cannot have an answer for what it is not the author of.

- God is the Author and He has the answer to every problem.

- If you ignore the Author, you cannot prosper.

3 John 1:2 BSB

"Beloved, I pray that in every way you may prosper and enjoy good health, as your soul also prospers."

- Without understanding who we are as sons of God, we do not have access to the answers we need here on earth.

Galatians 4:1 GWT

"Let me explain further. As long as an heir is a child, he is no better off than a slave, even though he owns everything."

Ecclesiastes 10:5-7 MSG

"Here's a piece of bad business I've seen on this earth, an error that can be blamed on whoever is in charge: Immaturity is given a place of prominence, while maturity is made to take a backseat. I've seen unproven upstarts riding in style, while experienced veterans are put out to pasture."

- When God's purpose is performed, glory is released. When God's purpose is not performed, you have dysfunction.

- Evil means to be out of order or dysfunctional.

Genesis 2:18-20 BSB

"The LORD God also said, "It is not good for the man to be alone. I will make for him a suitable helper."
And out of the ground the LORD God formed every beast of the field and every bird of the air, and He brought them to the man to see what he would name each one. And whatever the man called each living creature, that was its name.
The man gave names to all the livestock, to the birds of the air, and to every beast of the field. But for Adam no suitable helper was found."

- Revelation from God is necessary for the fulfillment of our purpose.

Deuteronomy 29:29 BSB

"The secret things belong to the LORD our God, but the things revealed belong to us and to our children forever, so that we may follow all the words of this law."

- Creation must recognize God's image and likeness in us, so **that it obeys us.**

Romans 8:19 ESV

"For the creation waits with eager longing for the revealing of the sons of God"

Questions for Lesson 7

1. Who is the Author of the universe?
   _____
   _____
   _____

2. Who has the answers for the world's problems?
   _____
   _____
   _____

3. What stops us from prospering?
   _____
   _____
   _____

4. What happens when we don't know who we are?
   _____
   _____
   _____

5. What happens when God's purpose is performed?
   _____
   _____
   _____

6. What happens when God's purpose is not performed?
_____
_____
_____

7. What do we need from God to fulfill our purpose?
_____
_____
_____

⭐ **Puzzle 5**

Make your way through the maze and receive your own crown.

Start Here

Finish Here

Kingdom Curriculum for Kids: God's Image

Lesson 8   Law of Like Kind

- All life can only reproduce itself.

Genesis 1:11-12, 21, 24, 26 BSB

"Then God said, "Let the earth bring forth vegetation: seed-bearing plants and fruit trees, each bearing fruit with seed according to its kind." And it was so. The earth produced vegetation: seed-bearing plants according to their kinds and trees bearing fruit with seed according to their kinds. And God saw that it was good."

"So God created the great sea creatures and every living thing that moves, with which the waters teemed according to their kinds, and every bird of flight after its kind. And God saw that it was good."

"And God said, "Let the earth bring forth living creatures according to their kinds: livestock, land crawlers, and beasts of the earth according to their kinds." And it was so."

"Then God said, "Let Us make man in Our image, after Our likeness, to rule over the fish of the sea and the birds of the air, over the livestock, and over all the earth itself and every creature that crawls upon it."

- The earth tells the truth because it is governed by laws.

Psalm 119:91 NIV

"Your laws endure to this day, for all things serve you"

Jeremiah 31:35 ISV

"This is what the LORD says, who gives the sun for light by day, the laws that govern the moon and stars for light by night, and who stirs up the sea so that its waves roar. The LORD of the Heavenly Armies is his name:"

Jeremiah 33:25 GNT

"But I, the LORD, have a covenant with day and night, and I have made the laws that control earth and sky."

- The earth was never intended to operate independent of Heaven. We need God in our lives.

Psalm 8 NLT

"O LORD, our Lord, your majestic name fills the earth!
  Your glory is higher than the heavens.
You have taught children and infants to tell of your strength,
silencing your enemies and all who oppose you.
When I look at the night sky and see the work of your fingers—
the moon and the stars you set in place—
what are mere mortals that you should think about them,
  human beings that you should care for them?
Yet you made them only a little lower than God
  and crowned them with glory and honor.
You gave them charge of everything you made,
  putting all things under their authority—

*the flocks and the herds and all the wild animals,
the birds in the sky, the fish in the sea, and everything that swims the ocean currents.
O LORD, our Lord, your majestic name fills the earth!"*

- We were made in God's image and likeness to operate as His representative here in the earth.

- When the purpose of a thing is fulfilled, a glory is released.

- Men and women were created to fulfill God's ultimate purpose in the earth.

- It takes both men and women working together for this purpose to be accomplished.

Genesis 1:26-28 BSB

*"Then God said, "Let Us make man in Our image, after Our likeness, to rule over the fish of the sea and the birds of the air, over the livestock, and over all the earth itself and every creature that crawls upon it."
So God created man in His own image; in the image of God He created him; male and female He created them.
God blessed them and said to them, "Be fruitful and multiply, and fill the earth and subdue it; rule over the fish of the sea and the birds of the air and every creature that crawls upon the earth.""*

Mark 10:6 GWT

"But God made them male and female in the beginning, at creation."

Genesis 2:18-24 BSB

"The LORD God also said, "It is not good for the man to be alone. I will make for him a suitable helper." And out of the ground the LORD God formed every beast of the field and every bird of the air, and He brought them to the man to see what he would name each one. And whatever the man called each living creature, that was its name. The man gave names to all the livestock, to the birds of the air, and to every beast of the field. But for Adam no suitable helper was found. So the LORD God caused the man to fall into a deep sleep, and while he slept, He took one of the man's ribs and closed up the area with flesh. And from the rib that the LORD God had taken from the man, He made a woman and brought her to him. And the man said: "This is now bone of my bones and flesh of my flesh; she shall be called 'woman,' for out of man she was taken." For this reason a man will leave his father and mother and be united to his wife, and they will become one flesh."

- Anything operating outside of its purpose is perverted.

- When man walks away from God's purpose for his life, he establishes his own purposes resorting to his fallen nature instead of to God.

- We must have our minds transformed by the truth of God's Word.

Romans 12:2 BSB

"Do not be conformed to this world, but be transformed by the renewing of your mind. Then you will be able to test and approve what is the good, pleasing, and perfect will of God."

Questions for Lesson 8

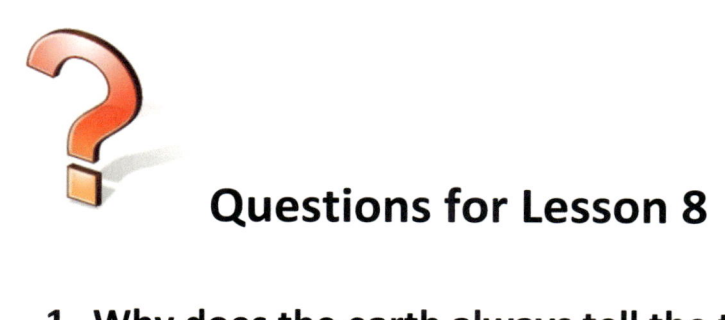

1. Why does the earth always tell the truth?
   _____
   _____
   _____

2. Who do we need in our lives?
   _____
   _____
   _____

3. Who was made in God's image and likeness?
   _____
   _____
   _____

4. Who was made to represent God in the earth?
   _____
   _____
   _____

5. What is released when purpose is fulfilled?
   _____
   _____
   _____

6. What were we created for?

   _____
   _____
   _____

7. Who has to work together for God's purpose to be fulfilled?

   _____
   _____
   _____

8. What is anything operating outside of its purpose?

   _____
   _____
   _____

Puzzle 6

Word Puzzle

Transform one word into another.
We go from being a …
<u>mere human</u>

_____ add a letter "I" in front of
the letter "m" in the word mere

_____ remove the letters "h" & "u" in
the word human

_____ add the letters "o" & "f" and
leave a space between "of" & the
word man

_____ remove the letters "e" & "r" and
add the letters "a" & "g"

_____ remove the letter "n" from man
and add the letter "d"

_____ remove the letter "a" from mad
and add the letter "o"

to being transformed into the

_____ remove the letter "m" from mod
and add the capital letter "G"

Genesis 1:26
2 Corinthians 3:18
Romans 8:29

Kingdom Curriculum for Kids: God's Image

Lesson 9   God's Ultimate Purpose

- God's ultimate purpose is the manifestation of His Heavenly Kingdom here on earth in partnership with His sons.

- We have to yield to the supernatural power of God and participate in manifesting God's Heavenly culture in the earth.

- The Word of God is the provision God has given us to overcome this world's situations.

1 John 5:4 NIV

"for everyone born of God overcomes the world. This is the victory that has overcome the world, even our faith."

Revelation 21:7 BLB

"The one who overcomes will inherit all things, and I will be his God, and he will be My son."

1 John 4:4 BSB

"You, little children, are from God and have overcome them, because greater is He who is in you than he who is in the world." We must go past our minds.

Ephesians 4:23 CEV

"Let the Spirit change your way of thinking"

Romans 12:2 BSB

"Do not be conformed to this world, but be transformed by the renewing of your mind. Then you will be able to test and approve what is the good, pleasing, and perfect will of God".

Colossians 3:10 NLT

"Put on your new nature, and be renewed as you learn to know your Creator and become like him."

- We have to understand who and what we are.

1 John 3:2 KJV

"Beloved, now are we the sons of God, and it doth not yet appear what we shall be: but we know that, when he shall appear, we shall be like him; for we shall see him as he is."

Romans 8:16 ABIPE

"And that Spirit testifies to our spirit that we are sons of God;"

- We find out who we are through the Word of God.

- Law of Revelation

- If God reveals to man that which he could not know by any other means, then that revelation is necessary for man to fulfill his purpose.

Deuteronomy 29:29 ESV

"The secret things belong to the LORD our God, but the things that are revealed belong to us and to our children forever, that we may do all the words of this law."

Questions for Lesson 9

1. How do we participate in manifesting God's Heavenly culture in the earth?

   _____
   _____
   _____

2. What is the provision that God has given us to overcome this world's situations?

   _____
   _____
   _____

3. What should we not be limited to?

   _____
   _____
   _____

4. What do we need to understand?

   _____
   _____
   _____

5. How do we find out who we are?

   _____
   _____
   _____

6. What is necessary for us to know in order for us to fulfill our purpose?
_____
_____
_____

7. What verse explains the Law of Revelation?
_____
_____
_____

Puzzle 7

Find your way to the center of the maze.

Proverbs 25:2 ABIPE

Kingdom Curriculum for Kids: God's Image

Lesson 10   What is Man?: God's Voice in the Earth

Genesis 1:26 KJV

"And God said, Let us make man in our image, after our likeness: and let them have dominion over the fish of the sea, and over the fowl of the air, and over the cattle, and over all the earth, and over every creeping thing that creepeth upon the earth."

Genesis 2:7 KJV

"And the LORD God formed man of the dust of the ground, and breathed into his nostrils the breath of life; and man became a living soul."

- Creation and formation of man lets you know that man is a combination of spirit and flesh.

- The real man is a speaking spirit, like God.

- God has given us dominion or His sovereign authority over territory as a provision for the advancement of His Kingdom.

- As sons of God, we have to operate supernaturally to supersede or overcome natural situations.

- Man has to exercise his authority over creation, just like God.

Romans 8:19 BSB

"The creation waits in eager expectation for the revelation of the sons of God."

- In order to exercise our authority, we must have the mind of Christ.

1 Corinthians 2:16 BSB

"For who has known the mind of the Lord, so as to instruct Him?" But we have the mind of Christ.

John 15:15 CEV

Servants don't know what their master is doing, and so I don't speak to you as my servants. I speak to you as my friends, and I have told you everything my Father has told me.

- Formation is taking material matter and forming something to fulfill purpose.

- This is what God did with man in Genesis 1:26-28 and 2:7.

- Both male and female have the image and likeness of God within them.

- Image refers to man's functional role rather than physical build.

- It takes both a male and female to fulfill God's purpose in the earth.

Genesis 4:1 GNT

"Then Adam had intercourse with his wife, and she became pregnant. She bore a son and said, "By the LORD's help I have gotten a son." So she named him Cain."

Questions for Lesson 10

1. What is man made of?

2. What makes man like God?

3. What has God given us to advance His Kingdom with?

4. How do we have to operate as sons of God?

5. What do we have to exercise over creation in order to be like God?

6. What do we have to have in order to exercise our authority?
_____
_____
_____

7. What is formation?
_____
_____
_____

8. What does image refer to?
_____
_____
_____

Puzzle 8

Word Scramble Puzzle 1

Unscramble the words using the scripture as a clue.

1. s n k g i   ___ ___ ___ ___ ___   Rev. 5:10

2. e o c n i t r a   ___ ___ ___ ___ ___ ___ ___ ___   Rom. 8:20

3. r e e k f w o n   ___ ___ ___ ___ ___ ___ ___ ___   Rom. 8:29

4. r d s i e p e e t n d   ___ ___ ___ ___ ___ ___ ___ ___ ___ ___ ___   Rom. 8:29

5. s n e d y t i   ___ ___ ___ ___ ___ ___ ___   Phil. 3:19 NIV

6. r e h r o b s t   ___ ___ ___ ___ ___ ___ ___ ___   Mk. 10:30

7. s r s s e t i   ___ ___ ___ ___ ___ ___ ___   Mk. 10:30

8. d m n i h a o s   ___ ___ ___ ___ ___ ___ ___ ___   Col. 3:16 BSB

9. i h y c l r   ___ ___ ___ ___ ___ ___   Col. 3:16 BSB

Kingdom Curriculum for Kids: God's Image

Lesson 11   Representation of God

- We are here to remind creation that we represent God and Heaven's culture here in the earth.

- We are representatives of God, here in the earth in the place of God, the Author and Creator.

2 Corinthians 5:20 NLT

"So we are Christ's ambassadors; God is making his appeal through us. We speak for Christ when we plead, "Come back to God!""

1 Corinthians 3:9 GWT

"We are God's coworkers. You are God's field. You are God's building."

- We assume the identity, power and authority of the one who sent us on assignment here in the earth.

- We become another speaking spirit, like God. God's work is to speak. Speaking is doing.

Revelation 12:11a KJV

"And they overcame him by the blood of the Lamb, and by the word of their testimony;"

Exodus 4:15-16 GNT

"You can speak to him and tell him what to say. I will help both of you to speak, and I will tell you both what to do. He will be your spokesman and speak to the people for you. Then you will be like God, telling him what to say."

- The world needs to hear God's voice through you.

Exodus 7:1 GNT

"The LORD said, "I am going to make you like God to the king, and your brother Aaron will speak to him as your prophet."

Questions for Lesson 11

1. Why are we here in the earth?
   _____
   _____
   _____

2. What do we assume from God while on assignment for Him?
   _____
   _____
   _____

3. What is God's work?
   _____
   _____
   _____

4. What does the world need to hear through you?
   _____
   _____
   _____

Puzzle 9

```
a b c d e f g h i j r k l m n o
p q r s t u x y v o u i y z a b
t u v w h x y z n a b c c d e c
s i h c a d m o n i s h g h f d
r j a k l m n n o p t q r s l e
q e d c b m a z y x w s v u t y
t f g h a i j k l m n o e p q f
p n e d a b e d e f g v h d i m
o l e r q p d o n m a l e k j o
n k m s u w b f x g s n m v a d
m j n s e c o w y e i g u w e s
l i o l t r e w z t s h t n b i
k h l z m n p v s a t l w x c w
j g p e k c d e b b e o s y o g
i f d e v r d v r c r j r r d h
h e r y w e e t o c s k l y e i
g o q x r a f s t h f d r z f j
f d r p x t k r h a e o q a g k
f c s w y i g q e r l l p b h l
e b t v n o h p r g d n o c i m
d a u g z n a o s e n m l k j n
c b s a z y x w v u t s r q p o
```

kings
creation
foreknew
predestined
destiny
brothers
sisters
admonish

dwell
teach
wisdom
world
made
formed
represent
crowned

honor
charge
gave
richly
glory

Kingdom Curriculum for Kids: God's Image

Lesson 12   Not Conforming to the Current Culture Pt.1

Roman 12:2 BSB

"Do not be conformed to this world, but be transformed by the renewing of your mind. Then you will be able to test and approve what is the good, pleasing, and perfect will of God."

- You must not allow what is popular in culture or the world to cause you to turn away from God's standards.

John 15:19 NIV

"If you belonged to the world, it would love you as its own. As it is, you do not belong to the world, but I have chosen you out of the world. That is why the world hates you"

2 Timothy 3:1-9 NLT

"You should know this, Timothy, that in the last days there will be very difficult times. For people will love only themselves and their money. They will be boastful and proud, scoffing at God,

disobedient to their parents, and ungrateful. They will consider nothing sacred. They will be unloving and unforgiving; they will slander others and have no self-control. They will be cruel and hate what is good. They will betray their friends, be reckless, be puffed up with pride, and love pleasure rather than God. They will act religious, but they will reject the power that could make them godly. Stay away from people like that!

They are the kind who work their way into people's homes and win the confidence of vulnerable women who are burdened with the guilt of sin and controlled by various desires. (Such women are forever following new teachings, but they are never able to understand the truth.) These teachers oppose the truth just as Jannes and Jambres opposed Moses. They have depraved minds and a counterfeit faith. But they won't get away with this for long. Someday everyone will recognize what fools they are, just as with Jannes and Jambres"

- As Kingdom citizens, we have been given a standard to live by that does not change based on man's customs and culture.

1 John 4:4-6 BSB

"You, little children, are from God and have overcome them, because greater is He who is in you than he who is in the world. They are of the world. That is why they speak from the world's perspective, and the world listens to them. We are from God. Whoever knows God listens to us; whoever is not from God does not listen to us. That is how we know the Spirit of truth and the spirit of deception."

Malachi 3:6a NLT

"I am the LORD, and I do not change."

Hebrews 13:8 BSB

"Jesus Christ is the same yesterday and today and forever."

- We are called to be light and salt in a dark and tasteless world.

Matthew 5:13-15 NLT

"You are the salt of the earth. But what good is salt if it has lost its flavor? Can you make it salty again? It will be thrown out and trampled underfoot as worthless. "You are the light of the world— like a city on a hilltop that cannot be hidden. No one lights a lamp and then puts it under a basket. Instead, a lamp is placed on a stand, where it gives light to everyone in the house."

Matthew 5:16 BSB

"In the same way, let your light shine before men, that they may see your good deeds and glorify your Father in heaven."

- In order do be light and salt, we must have our minds renewed with the Word of God.

Ephesians 4:23-24 BSB

"to be renewed in the spirit of your minds; and to put on the new self, created to be like God in true righteousness and holiness."

- As Kingdom citizens, we are responsible for being an example of God's Kingdom in the world.

Colossians 4:5 NLT

"Live wisely among those who are not believers, and make the most of every opportunity."

1 John 5:4 BSB

"because everyone born of God overcomes the world. And this is the victory that has overcome the world: our faith."

- We are to be bearers of truth in a world that has exchanged the truth for a lie.

Romans 1:16-32 BSB

"I am not ashamed of the gospel, because it is the power of God for salvation to everyone who believes, first to the Jew, then to the Greek. For the gospel reveals the righteousness of God that comes by faith from start to finish, just as it is written: "The righteous will live by faith." The wrath of God is being revealed from heaven against all the godlessness and wickedness of men who suppress the truth by their wickedness. For what may be known about God is plain to them, because God has made it plain to them. For since the creation of the world God's invisible qualities, His eternal power and divine nature, have been clearly seen, being understood from His workmanship, so that men are without excuse. For although they knew God, they neither glorified Him as God nor gave thanks to Him, but they became futile in their thinking and darkened in their foolish hearts. Although they claimed to be wise, they became fools, and exchanged the glory of the immortal God for images of

mortal man and birds and animals and reptiles. Therefore God gave them over in the desires of their hearts to impurity for the dishonoring of their bodies with one another. They exchanged the truth of God for a lie, and worshiped and served the creature rather than the Creator, who is forever worthy of praise! Amen.

For this reason God gave them over to dishonorable passions. Even their women exchanged natural relations for unnatural ones. Likewise, the men abandoned natural relations with women and burned with lust for one another. Men committed indecent acts with other men, and received in themselves the due penalty for their error. Furthermore, since they did not see fit to acknowledge God, He gave them up to a depraved mind, to do what ought not to be done. They have become filled with every kind of wickedness, evil, greed, and depravity. They are full of envy, murder, strife, deceit, and malice. They are gossips, slanderers, God-haters, insolent, arrogant, and boastful. They invent new forms of evil; they disobey their parents. They are senseless, faithless, heartless, merciless. Although they know God's righteous decree that those who do such things are worthy of death, they not only continue to do these things, but also approve of those who practice them."

- As Kingdom citizens and ambassadors, we are responsible for representing God and His standards in the earth.

1 John 5:3 GWT

"To love God means that we obey his commandments. Obeying his commandments isn't difficult"

Daniel 1:3-9 NLT

"Then the king ordered Ashpenaz, his chief of staff, to bring to the palace some of the young men of Judah's royal family and other noble families, who had been brought to Babylon as captives "Select only strong, healthy, and good-looking young men," he said. "Make sure they are well versed in every branch of learning, are gifted with knowledge and good judgment, and are suited to serve in the royal palace. Train these young men in the language and literature of Babylon." The king assigned them a daily ration of food and wine from his own kitchens. They were to be trained for three years, and then they would enter the royal service. Daniel, Hananiah, Mishael, and Azariah were four of the young men chosen, all from the tribe of Judah. The chief of staff renamed them with these Babylonian names: Daniel was called Belteshazzar. Hananiah was called Shadrach. Mishael was called Meshach. Azariah was called Abednego. But Daniel was determined not to defile himself by eating the food and wine given to them by the king. He asked the chief of staff for permission not to eat these unacceptable foods. Now God had given the chief of staff both respect and affection for Daniel."

Questions for Lesson 12

1. What is it that we must not allow?
   _____
   _____
   _____

2. As Kingdom citizens, what do we live by?
   _____
   _____
   _____

3. What are we called to be to the world?
   _____
   _____
   _____

4. What do we need in order to be light and salt?
   _____
   _____
   _____

5. As Kingdom citizens, what are we responsible for?
   _____
   _____
   _____

6. What are we bearers of to the world?

_____
_____
_____

7. Who and what do we represent in the earth?

_____
_____
_____

Puzzle 10

Word Scramble Puzzle 2

Unscramble the words using the scripture as a clue.

1. s o r u p e p ___ ___ ___ ___ ___ ___ ___ Hebrews 6:17 BSB

2. o h y t u ___ ___ ___ ___ ___ 2 Timothy 2:22 NIV

3. r l e c a ___ ___ ___ ___ ___ Revelation 4:6 NIV

4. gdtenuiasnrnd __ __ __ __ __ __ __ __ __ __ __
   Proverbs 1:2 KJV

5. m g i d o k n ___ ___ ___ ___ ___ ___ ___ Mark 3:24

6. v t e s e e i c p r p __ __ __ __ __ __ __ __ __ __ __
   1 John 4:5 BSB

7. r e t s e y y a d __ __ __ __ __ __ __ __ __ Hebrews 13:8

8. g n l a c e l e h __ __ __ __ __ __ __ __ __ Job 9:19 NIV

9. o w o r o t r m __ __ __ __ __ __ __ Numbers 16:5 BSB

Kingdom Curriculum for Kids: God's Image

Lesson 13   Not Conforming to the Current Culture Pt.2

Romans 12:2 BSB

"Do not be conformed to this world, but be transformed by the renewing of your mind. Then you will be able to test and approve what is the good, pleasing, and perfect will of God."

- We do not operate by our personal opinions, but by what the King has said. God is our King.

John 12:49 NLT

"I don't speak on my own authority. The Father who sent me has commanded me what to say and how to say it."

- We need to use our influence to show people a better way.

1 Peter 3:15 CSB

"but in your hearts regard Christ the Lord as holy, ready at any time to give a defense to anyone who asks you for a reason for the hope that is in you"

- We use our lives as an example of the Kingdom's culture.

1 Peter 2:12 CEV & GWT

"Always let others see you behaving properly, even though they may still accuse you of doing wrong. Then on the day of judgment, they will honor God by telling the good things they saw you do."

"Live decent lives among unbelievers. Then, although they ridicule you as if you were doing wrong while they are watching you do good things, they will praise God on the day he comes to help you."

- We have to watch out for the pressure that would cause us to compromise.

1 John 2:15 NLT

"Do not love this world nor the things it offers you, for when you love the world, you do not have the love of the Father in you"

James 4:4 CEV

"You people aren't faithful to God! Don't you know if you love the world, you are God's enemies? And if you decide to be a friend of the world, you make yourself an enemy of God."

Daniel 3:16-18 NLT

" Shadrach, Meshach, and Abednego replied, "O Nebuchadnezzar, we do not need to defend ourselves before you. If we are thrown into the blazing furnace, the God whom we serve is able to save us. He will rescue us from your power, Your Majesty

But even if he doesn't, we want to make it clear to you, Your Majesty, that we will never serve your gods or worship the gold statue you have set up."

- We cannot back down our standard of morality to make people feel comfortable or okay about ungodly choices.

Ezekiel 3:17-19 BSB

"Son of man, I have made you a watchman for the house of Israel. Whenever you hear a word from My mouth, give them a warning from Me. If you say to the wicked man, 'You will surely die,' <u>but you do not warn him or speak out to warn him from his wicked way to save his life, that wicked man will die in his iniquity, and I will hold you responsible for</u> his blood. But if you warn a wicked man and he does not turn from his wickedness and his wicked way, he will die in his iniquity, but you will have saved yourself...."

Ezekiel 33:6 BSB

"But if the watchman sees the enemy coming and doesn't sound the alarm to warn the people, he is responsible for their captivity. They will die in their sins, but I will hold the watchman responsible for their deaths.'"

- God holds us responsible for warning people who come across our path who are operating against His culture and standard.

Questions for Lesson 13

1. What do we need to avoid operating by?

   _____
   _____
   _____

2. What do we need to operate by?

   _____
   _____
   _____

3. What do we use our influence for?

   _____
   _____
   _____

4. How do we show people God's Kingdom culture?

   _____
   _____
   _____

5. What causes us to compromise that we have to watch out for?

   _____
   _____
   _____

6. What do we need to keep up regardless of how people feel about it?

_____
_____
_____

7. What does God hold us responsible for?

_____
_____
_____

Question Key for Lesson 1

1. What did God want to do with man?
God wanted to share His Kingdom.

2. What did God do with the earth before He put man on it?
God made the earth perfectly suited and ready for man to live on.

3. How did God make mankind?
God made man by speaking him into existence.

4. What did God provide for man on earth?
God provided everything man would need to live an abundant life.

5. How did Adam and Eve lose the Kingdom?
They made a choice to disobey God by eating the forbidden fruit.

6. What did Jesus come to do?
Jesus came to bring His Kingdom back into the earth and to make it available to man again.

7. How did Jesus restore God's Kingdom?
Jesus died and made the sacrifice that was necessary to cleanse man from his sin.

8. How can you enter the Kingdom of God?
You must receive Jesus as your Savior.

Question Key for Lesson 2

1. When you become a Kingdom citizen, what are your rights?
You have a right to protection, provision and purpose.

2. What do you become in God's family?
You become a son of God.

3. What does the word <u>man</u> represent in the Kingdom of God?
Man represents mankind in which there are males and females.

4. What does the word <u>son</u> represent in the Kingdom of God?
The word son represents a family member in which there are sons and daughters.

5. Why did God make man male and female?
God made them that way on purpose in order to have both males and females fulfill specific purposes.

6. What are your responsibilities as a Kingdom citizen?
Your responsibilities are to obey the King, to be loyal to the King and to give to the King's Kingdom.

7. What is a reciprocal relationship?
It is a relationship where there is giving and receiving.

Question Key for Lesson 3

1. What do we need to understand when we are learning from the Bible?
We must understand what God's original plan was for us.

2. What is dominion?
Dominion is God's authority over territory; it is final and absolute.

3. What is authority?
Authority is the right to do as you wish with what you have authority over.

4. What is God's original plan?
God's original plan is the manifestation of His heavenly Kingdom here on earth in partnership with His sons and daughters.

5. Why did God make us like Him?
So that He could work with us and through us.

6. What allows us to be legal on the earth?
Our dirt body allows us to be legal on the dirt earth.

7. What qualifies us for dominion?
Image and likeness of God is what qualifies man for dominion.

Question Key for Lesson 4

1. Who are the representatives for God in the earth?
The born again sons of God are.

2. What is the definition of image?
Image is a visual representation or exact likeness of something.

3. What role does the image play?
When people see us, they should see the image of God.

4. What does it mean to be a representative of God?
We can act on God's behalf.

5. What does it mean to be a reflection of God?
We bring the presence of God wherever we go.

Question Key for Lesson 5

1. Do you know who you are?

2. Who did not know their identity in the Garden of Eden?
Adam and Eve did not know their identity.

3. Who came to earth to show us who we are?
Jesus did.

4. Are you able to engage the world successfully if you do not know who you are?
No.

5. What does the enemy use to challenge your identity?
The enemy uses twisted doctrine to challenge your identity.

Question Key for Lesson 6

1. What does man possess from God that allows him to partner with God?
Man possesses God's image and God's likeness.

2. Who was God speaking to in Genesis 1:26?
God was speaking to creation.

3. What does man revert or turn to when God is not in his life?
Man reverts or turns back to ignorance.

4. What is ignorance?
Ignorance is the failure to recognize available facts and information. You ignore what is obvious.

5. What does fallen man use to fashion or shape his identity?
Man uses his fallen imagination to fashion or shape his identity.

Question Key for Lesson 7

1. Who is the Author of the universe?
God is the Author of the universe.

2. Who has the answers for the world's problems?
God, The Author has the answers for the world's problems.

3. What stops us from prospering?
Ignoring the Author stops us from prospering.

4. What happens when we don't know who we are?
We do not have access to the answers we need.

5. What happens when God's purpose is performed?
When God's purpose is performed, glory is released.

6. What happens when God's purpose is not performed?
When God's purpose is not performed, you have dysfunction.

7. What do we need from God to fulfill our purpose?
We need revelation from God to fulfill our purpose.

Question Key for Lesson 8

1. Why does the earth always tell the truth?
The earth tells the truth because it is governed by laws.

2. Who do we need in our lives?
We need God in our lives.

3. Who was made in God's image and likeness?
We were made in God's image and likeness.

4. Who was made to represent God in the earth?
We were made to represent God in the earth.

5. What is released when purpose is fulfilled?
Glory is released when purpose is fulfilled.

6. What were we created for?
We were created to fulfill God's ultimate purpose in the earth.

7. Who has to work together for God's purpose to be fulfilled?
Both men and women have to work together for God's purpose to be fulfilled.

8. What is anything operating outside of its purpose?
Anything operating outside of its purpose is perverted.

Question Key for Lesson 9

1. How do we participate in manifesting God's Heavenly culture in the earth?
We have to yield to or allow the supernatural power of God to work through us to manifest God's Heavenly culture.

2. What is the provision that God has given us to overcome this world's situations?
God has given us His Word.

3. What should we not be limited to?
We should not be limited to our minds.

4. What do we need to understand?
We need to understand who and what we are.

5. How do we find out who we are?
We find out who we are through the Word of God.

6. What is necessary for us to know in order for us to fulfill our purpose?
We need to know the Law of Revelation in order for us to fulfill our purpose.

7. What verse explains the Law of Revelation?
Deuteronomy 29:29 explains the Law of Revelation.

Question Key for Lesson 10

1. What is man made of?
Man is a combination of spirit and flesh.

2. What makes man like God?
Man is a speaking spirit like God.

3. What has God given us to advance His Kingdom with?
God has given us dominion or His sovereign authority over territory.

4. How do we have to operate as sons of God?
We have to operate supernaturally to supersede or overcome natural situations.

5. What do we have to exercise over creation in order to be like God?
We have to exercise our authority over creation.

6. What do we have to have in order to exercise our authority?
We must have the mind of Christ in order to exercise our authority.

7. What is formation?
Formation is taking material matter and forming something to fulfill purpose.

8. What does image refer to?
Image refers to man's functional role rather than physical build.

Question Key for Lesson 11

1. Why are we here in the earth?
We are here to remind creation that we represent God and Heaven's culture here in the earth.

2. What do we assume from God while on assignment for Him?
We assume the identity, power and authority of the One who sent us on assignment here in the earth.

3. What is God's work?
God's work is to speak.

4. What does the world need to hear through you?
The world needs to hear God's voice through you.

Question Key for Lesson 12

1. What is it that we must not allow?
We must not allow what is popular in culture or the world to cause us to turn away from God's standards.

2. As Kingdom citizens, what do we live by?
We live by a standard that does not change based on man's customs and culture.

3. What are we called to be to the world?
We are called to be light and salt in a dark and tasteless world.

4. What do we need in order to be light and salt?
We need to have our minds renewed with the Word of God.

5. As Kingdom citizens, what are we responsible for?
We are responsible for being an example of God's Kingdom in the world.

6. What are we bearers of to the world?
We are bearers of truth in a world that has exchanged the truth for a lie.

7. Who and what do we represent in the earth?
We represent God and His standards in the earth.

Question Key for Lesson 13

1. What do we need to avoid operating by?
We need to avoid operating by our personal opinions.

2. What do we need to operate by?
We need to operate by God's Word.

3. What do we use our influence for?
We need to use our influence to show people a better way.

4. How do we show people God's Kingdom culture?
We show people God's Kingdom culture by using our lives as an example.

5. What causes us to compromise that we have to watch out for?
We have to watch out for pressure that would cause us to compromise.

6. What do we need to keep up regardless of how people feel about it?
We need to keep up God's standard of morality.

7. What does God hold us responsible for?
We are responsible for warning people who come across our path who are operating against His culture and standard.

Puzzle 1 Key

```
a b c d e f g y h i j k l i m u
b n o p q r s a t u v w x m y n
c z a b c d e d f g h i j a k d
d l m n o p q r r s t u v g w e
e x y z z a b e c d e c l e a r
w o r r o m o t h f g h i g j s
f r h o k l m s n o p q r s t t
g i i p u v i e w x y z a b c a
h g j q a f k y x f n d e f l n
i i c r e d a t y g a h i j i d
j n u s s d l c z o v c k l k i
k a l y o u t h m n i p e k e n
l l t t p e n a v i g a t i n g
m a u t r f m l q r a s t n e u
n s r u u q n l v w t x y g s z
o b e v p g o e a f e o n d s b
p c k m n o i n i m o d a o a c
q d l w i h p g b g k p l m d e
r e e v i t c e p s r e p w f g
s f m x b i q u c h l q t x h i
t g n y c j r v d i m r u y j k
u v w x y z s w e j n s v z l m
```

purpose
youth
clear
understanding
kingdom
perspective
navigating
challenge

face
times
culture
today
yesterday
tomorrow
image
original

likeness
dominion
fish
navigate
plan

Puzzle 3 Key

```
a b d f h j a l e s s o n s l n
c c n a b e c d c e f g t h i j
e d o k s l m n n o p h q r s t
g e p u r v w x e y g n i h t z
i f q a e u h v i i a b c d e f
k g r b t y t i r o h t u a g h
m h s c h v i w e i j k l g m n
o h t d g w j x p o p q r n s t
p i t r u x k y x u v w x i y z
q g u p a r t n e r s h i p a b
r n v e d e l o z k p z c e d e
s i w r l y m i a l q f g e h i
t n x c m z n t b e r j k r l y
u r y e n a o a c l l m n c o l
v a z p o b p t d b s t p q r n
w e e t p c q s e i t s t t u e
x l f i q d r e f s u v w a x v
y j g b l w o f g i v r y z c a
z k h l r e s i n v i s i b l e
a l i e s f t n b m w o a a b h
e t u l o s b a i n x n c d e f
b m j k t g u m j o y s g h i j
```

sea	absolute	visible
fowl	authority	invisible
air	right	experience
cattle	manifestation	lessons
creeping	heavenly	perceptible
thing	partnership	
earth	sons	
learning	daughters	

93

Puzzle 4 Key

```
a v a b c d e f g h i j k l m n
b w o p q r d s t u v w x y z a
c x q l f n i h g f e d c b a b
d y r t i s r q p o n m l k j c
e z s m r u v a w x y z m a e d
f p t a s b c d p e f g l h i e
g o u p t o y n m p l l j i k f
h n v q b d r s t u o v w x v g
i h k r o w f d g w y i x z y e
j m i b r g e c n b a z n k a h
k l w g n i n n i g e b w t b i
l k x u h d l k k w m n i l c j
m j y h t e e l a x l r n m d k
n i z i g c s m e y i o d n e t
o h j a u b f t p p k p e o r l
p g l s v a y n s z j q e i f m
q f k r w f g o v e i r d r o w
r e l q i l h p u f n s v p g n
s d m l x e i q t g h s u q h o
t c a p y s n o i t o m e r i p
u u n o z h j r s u t u t s j q
q b a z y x w l l i w v u t s r
```

senses · live · appoint
work · dirt · firstborn
spirit · allow · highest
soul · legal · body
mind · qualify · indeed
will · speaking
emotions · beginning
flesh · word

Puzzle 9 Key

a	b	c	d	e	f	g	h	i	j	r	k	l	m	n	o
p	q	r	s	t	u	x	y	v	o	u	i	y	z	a	b
t	u	v	w	h	x	y	z	n	a	b	c	c	d	e	c
s	i	h	c	a	d	m	o	n	i	s	h	g	h	f	d
r	j	a	k	l	m	h	n	o	p	t	q	r	s	l	e
q	e	d	c	b	m	a	z	y	x	w	s	v	u	t	y
t	f	g	h	a	i	j	k	l	m	n	o	e	p	q	f
p	n	e	d	a	b	e	d	e	f	g	v	h	d	i	m
o	l	e	r	q	p	d	o	n	m	a	l	e	k	j	o
n	k	m	s	u	w	b	f	x	g	s	n	m	v	a	d
m	j	n	s	e	c	o	w	y	e	i	g	u	w	e	s
l	i	o	l	t	r	e	w	z	t	s	h	t	n	b	i
k	h	l	z	m	n	p	v	s	a	t	l	w	x	c	w
j	g	p	e	k	c	d	e	b	b	e	o	s	y	o	g
i	f	d	e	v	r	d	v	r	c	r	j	r	r	d	h
h	e	r	y	w	e	e	t	o	c	s	k	l	y	e	i
g	o	q	x	r	a	f	s	t	h	f	d	r	z	f	j
f	d	r	p	x	t	k	r	h	a	e	o	q	a	g	k
f	c	s	w	y	i	g	q	e	r	l	l	p	b	h	l
e	b	t	v	n	o	h	p	r	g	d	n	o	c	i	m
d	a	u	g	z	n	a	o	s	e	n	m	l	k	j	n
c	b	s	a	z	y	x	w	v	u	t	s	r	q	p	o

kings dwell honor
creation teach charge
foreknew wisdom gave
predestined world richly
destiny made glory
brothers formed
sisters represent
admonish crowned

Puzzle 8 Key

Word Scramble Puzzle 1

Unscramble the words using the scripture as a clue.

1. s n k g i   kings   Rev. 5:10

2. e o c n i t r a   creation   Rom. 8:20

3. r e e k f w o n   foreknew   Rom. 8:29

4. r d s i e p e e t n d   predestined   Rom. 8:29

5. s n e d y t i   destIny   Phil. 3:19 NIV

6. r e h r o b s t   brothers   Mk. 10:30

7. s r s s e t i   sisters   Mk. 10:30

8. d m n i h a o s   admonIsh   Col. 3:16 BSB

9. i h y c l r   richly   Col. 3:16 BSB

Puzzle 10 Key

Word Scramble Puzzle 2

Unscramble the words using the scripture as a clue.

1. s o r u p e p   **purpose**   Hebrews 6:17 BSB

2. o h y t u   **youth**   2 Timothy 2:22 NIV

3. r l e c a   **clear**   Revelation 4:6 NIV

4. gdtenuiasnrnd   **understanding**   Proverbs 1:2 KJV

5. m g i d o k n   **kingdom**   Mark 3:24

6. v t e s e e i c p r p   **perspectIve**

7. r e t s e y y a d   **yesterday**   1 John 4:5 BSB / Hebrews 13:8

8. g n l a c e l e h   **challenge**   Job 9:19 NIV

9. o w o r o t r m   **tomorrow**   Numbers 16:5 BSB

Made in United States
Troutdale, OR
09/07/2023